# Remnants of Warmth

Jeanne,
Am so happy to
share a love of the
north woods with
you!
— Best Regards,
Nancy Austin

# Remnants of Warmth

Poems by

Nancy Austin

Kelsay Books

Cover photograph: Nancy Austin

Author photograph: Mic Austin

ISBN 13: 978-0692579367

*Kelsay Books*
Aldrich Press
www.kelsaybooks.com

*To my north woods writing group:*

August's blue moon casts
a strand of pearls shoreward
a faded rose leans in

*Thanks for your revitalizing comradery and encouragement.*
*Thanks for gathering me in.*

*A thank you to my husband and to my family.*

*To Linda and Sue: Thanks for listening to so many poems.*
*A noi tre, sorelle per sempre!*

# Acknowledgements

A kind acknowledgement to the editors of the literary journals or publications listed below for publishing these, or earlier versions of the following poems:

*Adanna:* "Familial Rain"

*Ariel Anthology 2015*: "Fire Dragon of Change", "Lineage"

*Midwestern Gothic:* "Stories from Katie's Funeral"

*The Artist's Muse Traveling Exhibit:* "The Grace Within", "The Embrace of a Moment" and "What Nature Knows"

*Sheepshead Review:* "Hometown"

*Verse Wisconsin:* "What I Learned in 5th Grade", "BeaBlossom Inn", and "Poetry Class"

*Wisconsin Poets' Calendars*: "Old Firewood", "August's Blue Moon"

# Contents

# What I Learned in Fifth Grade

I befriended Sarah the summer
before my new school began.
Her family readily absorbed me,
like another helping of whipped potatoes
and steaming beef-tips, accepted with a nod
around their  wood-chipped farm table,
below the sticky curl of fly tape.

Sister Anna encouraged shy
but delighted oration with
*Our new student has poetic potential.*
Finished, I glanced up and saw
middle fingers extended upward
on outstretched arms,
when she wasn't looking.
The sea of green plaid shifted
and swirled into the walls,
pulled desks, chairs, ceiling, my air
into the crescendo of a silent tsunami,
lifted my feet, pushed me down,
rendered me invisible.

Maggie was her name.
Four or more followed her
every command.
Now, I saw Sarah was invisible too.
Yet somehow they noticed
her jet black hair stand out
against her pallid skin,
startled blue-topaz eyes,
wobbly, fawn-like legs.
Maggie and the four or more
pushed her face up against
cold black and white tiles,

and defiant of the sun-filled
bathroom windows,
smeared Chapstick in her hair.

In the dimly lit halls
Sarah walked stiffly,
whimpered softly,
as they poked pins
into her arms, her back, her butt.
They stood knock-kneed in a line
as she came out for recess,
wide-eyed and slow,
like cattle on the ramp
of a slaughterhouse.
They whispered, from desks behind,
things that made big tears jump
from her bowed, motionless head
onto the smeared glass of her wire rims,
collect, and rush down
the flush of her salt-dried cheeks.

Father James, the sisters, and lay teachers
were invisible too.
Maggie and the four or more
flicked paint at the back
of Sister Anna's habit,
staged sit-ins in the foyer, after recess.
One day the gate was open to Maggie's
neighborhood, and my parents drove in.
I heard them say
*Look, a groundskeeper!*
*You know, it wouldn't be such a*
*good church and school without*
*their generous contributions.*

14

# A Teen's Gift to a Therapist

After the long polishing process
I opened the rock tumbler
and palmed the once rough, raw stones:

    carnelian agates—cumulus clouds afloat on mud puddles

    tiger's eye—pulled taffy, butterscotch /vanilla

    spotted sodalite—glazed blue porcelain patterns on white china.

I placed these in the base of a clear glass flowerpot,
stared awhile, then covered them with soil.

The next layer:

    sunstone sparked with flashes of mica and metal

    jasper landscapes shape shifting desert to ocean

    common colored quartz polished to green aventurine.

Again I stared, concealed the stones with dirt
that funneled down the sides to reinforce the glass vessel.

Holding up the offering I could see
a polished glint, a hint of color,
a trace of fertile scent from
the iris bulb buried inside
—all signs of a willingness to bloom.

# Poetry Class

Another anonymous student
faced forward, sat stoically,
stared sleepily, fifty-five minutes,
three mornings per week.
A Native American,
never noticed, until not there.

The khaki-clad professor of
environmental science
explained you died
in a car wreck, the night before.
He offered no moment of silence,
just science.

I looked out the window
to ponder and day dream
an imagined life.
A mourning dove landed
on the thick cement window sill,
picked loudly at the glass divide
beside your empty chair.
I marveled and goose-bumped,
looked around to meet
a knowing glance or two,
but found none.
The beige vertical blinds
snapped shut by the professor
swung back and forth
exposing rapid snapshots,
final, feathered glimpses.

If this were my
poetry class,
we all would have
known it was you.
We would have
invited you in.

# Hometown

Bolting around the lofty, splintered fence,
no one dared the backwards glance,
sweaty swimsuits sticking under uncomfortable clothes,
formidable, red brick structure, lackluster,
larger than life, dwarfed by principal Beatty's
admonishing glare hovering over Mahtomedi Street.
The bulge of his crimson veins on balding red temples
traveled serpentine through a riot of freckles,
a Norman Rockwell gone awry.

The shoulder raising jolt of fear
melted with the rise and fall of Neptune Street,
nostrils flared with freshly cooled air,
eyes filled with the deepest dark blue
of White Bear Lake.

Always to old Ewald Brunner's dock,
sure to be at the VFW,
bony fingers racing over accordion keys.
Sure to be at all occasions
like Fred and Elna's fiftieth.
You never saw so much cheese.
Carefully cubed Colby and cheddar
mounded in crystal-cut bowls at table's end,
sticky-thick spreads flanked by stale crackers,
and little Willy Zuwicky wailing
mistaking his chubby, cheese coated finger
for yet another Cheetos.

# The Beablossom Inn, Lost River, Wisconsin

***** (1 of 1 review)

I'm not from here, of course, but a lucky break with
an overheated radiator led me to this delightful 5 star resort!
The Beablossom Inn's original amenities—chartreuse shag
carpeting, and ecru hobnail bedspreads (with popcorn accents)
are surprisingly clean! All six rooms have color TV's,
trusty plumbing, and Perfect Sleeper beds.
Jade shellback chairs, and a cushioned glider line the tourist court,
overlooking the coneflower garden. Purple poppy mallow frames
the stucco entrance. Yes, gas and groceries are 30 miles away,
but gracious owners Bea and Walter are famous for their
peanut butter and dill pickle sandwiches. Enjoy one in the lobby,
under vintage peacock drapes from the Ritz-Carlton, and Bea's
spoon collection, encased in glass.
Lost River was founded by Walter's great-grandfather,
and is crime free (except for Otto and Selma's son, Odis T.).
Located next to the Free Methodist Church, 20 miles off of I-70.
Look for our vintage sign (the odist may be missing again),
and the flashing orange neon arrow. Drug addicts not welcome.

# Stage Four of Four

The flip of the switch
sent blinding fluorescence
into the image
held tenuously up to
the scan of your eyes.

The darkened clot,
an eclipsed moon,
blocked the sun,
seized your voice.
stole your world.

# Familial Rain

My mother's glossy-green schefflera
had tousled leaves that bounced in the breeze
like her once-full head of hair.
*A schefflera in the wild is an epiphyte,*
*a plant that grows on another for support*
she explained, as she palmed
the bluish-brown spots that covered
its umbrella-like leaves.
She folded her mottled hands.
*Its sustenance comes from air, from rain*
she told me, eyes fixed on mine.
They both began to die as
my daughter was growing inside me.

I took a cutting from the last healthy stem,
and stored her Jardinière stoneware planter
in the garage.
The cutting from its mother plant,
became statuesque, its leaflets like
dancing stars in the window breeze.
Grandma, mom, an uncle, an aunt
died midway through their lives, as did
this commemorative plant,
consumed by the familiar spots.

Now, decades later, a cousin has died.
I retrieved the Jardinière pot,
placed a lush schefflara in the corner window
to glean the late afternoon sun.
Together, we lean into the light

to take sustenance in the
sweet-scented humidity
that hangs in the air
before the uneasy echo
of familial rain.

# Partings

**Part I**
You stood there
arms folded across your chest
below the banter of blue eyes,
like that looming, disapproving statue
we swore flashed a smile.
I could always read your expressions,
garner your approval,
like the time we ate at Beeliner's.
Spicy salsa squirted from your
black bean burrito, and splattered
onto your sensible white shirt,
your laundry lightened Levis.
You wished we could depart unnoticed,
like a cat when there's company,
surprised at my suggestion
to stay until it slowed.
Didn't you know I would stay forever?
The pungent smell of dried, red peppers
cascaded from ropes above,
like a ripe promise suspended
in the heat-thickened air.
My God, your blue eyes.

**Part II**
A faint footprint on
a dropped, white envelope,
his name above a post office box,
a credit card bill inside.
In his briefcase, passwords to websites,
titles and words increasingly blurred,

a worn postcard from Misery
  —no, Missouri
*I love you*
*when will I see you?*

I blindly drove him into the ruinous sun
that had parched the wheat fields
lining his industrial park.
  Eighteen years,
  hands held,
  babies born,
  degrees earned,
  trips taken,
  how to tell the kids,
  who would I be now?
Startled by the noise, I noticed
a massive crop sprinkler
recklessly throw away its water
like it didn't care.
I drove toward the sound and
powered down his window.
Cold, hard water slapped his face,
his laundry lightened shirt,
his pressed pants.

# Stories from Katie's Funeral

Katie was a five foot, eleven inch triangle
of skinny ankles, heron-like legs, and broad shoulders.
The day she told her family she was hired at the mill,
her uncle threw down his fork, sneered
*I don't know you and you don't know me,*
shot up from his chair, and started his car.

Katie was one of the first five women hired.
She was assigned to monitor slime-forming microbes,
and aced everything in her job description.
They put urine soaked clothes in her locker,
plastered Playboy and Penthouse pictures all over it,
hung a bra on the outside, dropped tampons in her tea,
and grabbed her breasts when she walked by.
They unzipped their pants, and peed on the paper machines
when she inspected them.  Still, she looked them in the eye
as she admonished, *Slime formers hang on everything.*
Katie never squealed on her Union brothers,
even when transferred to the Utilities group,
due to *all the commotion she caused.*

Katie hoisted a Nesco loaded with sausage, bacon, eggs,
and her stellar fried potatoes onto the Utilities table
on her first day.  She told them if they brought sweet rolls,
she would bring her potatoes the next week.
She declared Tuesday *Hot Dog Day*, and if they brought
condiments and buns, she'd make her choke cherry cobbler.
Every other Thursday became *Polish Sausage
and Sauerkraut Day*, and no one wanted to miss that.
When the utilities men learned she fostered a houseful
of troublesome kids, they chipped in for *Chinese Take-out Day*,
to give her a break.

Katie's clogged arteries caught up with her twenty-five years later.
Mill workers packed the funeral home.
A few of the old timers stood at the buffet line of steaming
Nescos, each with an apron and serving spoon.
They declared Saturday *Meatloaf in Memory of Katie Day.*

# Outfoxing the Fisher

They navigated the same ridges,
rocky outcrops, hollow logs
of this forested wetland.
She, a sly and clever thinker,
cat-like and agile,
had short legs that belied
sharp, seasoned teeth.
He, a competent climber,
young and muscular,
had mastered the ruthless,
relentless attack that left
a sharp, territorial scent.

Under the fullest of moons,
over luminous snow,
near the quorum of creatures
on the sinewy root mass
below the tallest black ash,
came the backlash.

She, tired of a lifetime
of snarls and lunges,
threats and posturing,
and guarding of kits,
stretched long her
soft, furry neck
and calmly exposed
her jugular.
He, ever keen
to advance his position,
to awe an audience,

pounced more vicious,
more visceral
than anyone could
have imagined.

The blood that
spurted and splattered
onto bright, white snow
drew gasps from flora and fauna,
and in disgust, they turned away.

# Old Baggage

I pull and drag this heavy trunk
weathered, time-honored, battered trunk,
it gets in my way wherever I go.
I have not looked inside it
for I know its contents by heart.
It's such a tedious trunk, unyielding trunk,
it gets in my way wherever I go.

One time I got a running head start,
ran forward with fortitude until hands struck
cold, rusty casings on cracked leather.
I pushed and pushed until it teetered
on the edge of a harrowing cliff,
mocking me, daring me, angering me.
It dropped like the huge, lead weight
it had been all those years.

It was quite expensive to have it exhumed.
Good thing it was a durable trunk, a dependable trunk.

# If You Have the Blues, Change Your Socks

Soft, squishy merino wool, cabled crews of mineral blue,
delphinium, Florida Keys, thick alpaca in cyan seas?

Try trouser socks in olive argyle, subtle stripes of crocodile,
mountain goat, Zinfandel, nectarine mist, woodsy chanterelle.

Basket weave anklets in honey-kissed, lily pink, lavender mist,
little lattice cuffs of lemon grass, hiking socks in freshwater bass.

Wools woven in silken strands, under tall boots, cashmere sands,
milky mohair in arctic fox, casual slouches of ruby-red phlox.

Knee-high socks in pumpkin vine, sleeping socks in winter's wine.
If you have the blues, change your socks.

# The Land I Live In

I live in the land of signs, white wooden arrows
nailed to trees, with painted remnants of Smith
or Schumacher, Loon's Nest or Bear's Den,
that point haphazardly down lanes
where creatures peer from the fringe of forests.

I live in the land of 50's vintage mom and pop resorts,
museums of memories, each on its own lake next to
another lake, and another, where beached boats nod
a welcome as tires crunch red granite drives
lined with swimsuits that summon from clotheslines.

I live in the land I've waited decades to call home,
where we off-loaded boats on legions of lakes
any warm weekend we could get away to navigate
shorelines, sit on sandbars knees-to-chin,
or tube through tannin-stained waves.

I live in the land where windows frame artwork,
"seasonals" escape cities, residents rally through
winter, grandkids gallop up driveways all smiles
and hugs, I live in the land where pitch of night
renders stargazers giddy and poets prolific.

# My Husband's Colonoscopy

He's tall, thick-bodied,
seriously straightforward,
bleeds eggs and bacon,
scoffs at the suggestion of scones.

In the waiting room of rides home
a 5 year-old flitted about, purple latex gloves
up to her armpits, scrub mask affixed,
surgery cap down to her nose.
One by one a nurse wheeled patients back,
laid out cold, to the maze of curtained cubicles.

A team brought out my husband.
Sitting upright, he waved his arms,
barked in basso profundo,
*Wheel me back and do the procedure.*
Their startled eyes met mine, eyebrows raised high.
*Watch this,* he bellowed, pulled off the oxygen sensor
and fixed his dark eyes on the opened cubicle curtain.
A young aide turned off the alarm
and stumbled as she hurried out.
As the blood pressure cuff innocently inflated
he thundered, *Watch this,* to no one in particular,
paused, then pumped his arm rigorously, fist clenched.
Several nurses removed it.
Eyes now closed, he lifted his head and shouted
*Atta big boy*, as the man behind the next curtain
expelled the air pumped into him for the procedure.
With one eye open, he hollered, *Great hang time*
at the next staccato cacophony.

Encouraged to leave early, we were warned
he would be groggy, would not remember anything.
We had the most enjoyable chamomile tea
and lavender-lemon scones on the way home.

# Networking on Vacation

My husband strode into the 100 year old
bed and breakfast bathroom,
magazine curled under his arm.
I prayed for a politely placed plunger,
exited to the Victorian sitting room,
and met an esteemed physician
whose wife worked in my profession.

Careful conversion was interrupted by a
*whooosh* that rang out repeatedly,
a rattle of pipes, just above.
I spoke louder with each assault,
until overtaken by a distinctive bellow
that bounced off the dried-out wooden walls,
*Be gone, you Damn, Dirty Demon,*
followed by a series of renewed flushes,
and the spirited approach
of footsteps down the staircase,
eager for an introduction.

# Fire Dragon of Change

Clock numbers glow,
they alternate,
cold flashes hot,
skin pendulates,
blankets tossed
high to acclimate,
in the dark, half asleep,
ancestral drums beat.

The meekness melts,
the violet shrinks
the mind to ancient
wisdom links.
I wade the stream,
I take a drink,
and birth sharp,
steaming, slapping wings.
Fearlessly sage,
deliciously strange,
behold the latest
warrior of change.

# Ask a Woman

if there is such a thing
as global warming
and she will say,
*What harm is there*
*in drinking water from a glass,*
*sharing a daily commute,*
*taking a brisk walk,*
*taking only what is needed?*
Ask a woman if there is such a thing
as climate change
and she will say,
*What harm is there*
*in tending indigenous gardens,*
*preserving lakes and streams,*
*protecting a fawn's nostril flare*
*to draw in crisp, clean air?*
Ask a woman to debate
such questions
and she will say,
*What harm is there*
*in maintaining coral reefs,*
*safeguarding ancestral forests,*
*loving people,*
*loving nature,*
*over things?*
*What soul, what society is not elevated*
*by a modicum of self-restraint?*
*Do we really need scores*
*of the latest mobile devices,*
*one and a half pound steaks,*
*and 29 flavors of pop-tarts?*

# Old Firewood

The new cord of firewood,
delivered today,
released its musky scent
as it tumbled from the truck bed.
Its dewy, fresh cut,
warm, wheat color,
and earthy aroma
delighted us.
We chuckled, such a discount
for ready to burn, solidly superior
to the old cord,
that shattered into shards
when it fell to the ground,
loosening lichen-spotted bark
from tough, twisted cores,
thus, unceremoniously stacked
in the corner.
We lowered three perfect logs
into the cold, cast iron stove,
pulled chairs forward
in smug anticipation,
lit them up, and waited.
They sputtered,
sizzled,
whistled,
but would not burn.

# Sent from My iPad

The pungency of a sharpened school bus-yellow pencil,
its facets felt in the roll of thumb and forefinger,
the graphite point as it catches on crisp linen paper,
scrap paper, gnarly bottom-of-purse paper,
the hand delivered paper airplane poem.

The pulpy nap of newsprint,
its dusky cast anointing the fingers,
the inky aura of a section thrown open,
the malleable, revered, dog-eared,
highlighted-to-hell favorite book.

The curled in bed cutting edge news,
the fresh thought, now read, written, delivered
on the cold glow of an iPad, tablet, e-Reader,
the mini flashlight, pen, and spiral notepad
gathering dust on the bedside table.

# The Grace Within

The landscape, at the end of the day
was awash with prospect,
like hands poised over a piano.
The water's calm coaxed the sun's rays
to skip like stones on her glassy plane,
a darting dance of diamonds.

With chair pulled close to the canvas
her hands became
the swoop of a swallow,
the bob of each blossom,
the deep wing beat of a heron,
the yearning in the tag alders and tamaracks,
the delight of the diaphanous clouds
waiting to uncover the moon.

# The Eraser

The high pitched bells of spring peepers,
trill of toads, and vibrato quack of a wood frog
saturated the dusk.
In the distance, a singular honk of a Canada goose,
here and there, oddly in the dark—as if circling the lake,
punctuated the night.

In the moments between dawn and daylight
when both mating frogs and birds are vocal,
came unusual chatter, pausing only
for the relentless honk of the lone goose,
a call akin to lamentation, unanswered
by its lifelong mate.
Something was off kilter, and the birds knew it,
*Phoebe-phoebe-phoebe* incited *teacher-teacher-teacher,*
and so on, into a hyperbolic pitch.
Even the chickadee's long and slow, high and low
could not restore order.

That morning a neighbor stopped by the garage.
*They call me the Eraser,* he boasted, as the limp neck
of a goose he clutched shook with his gesticulations.
*Shot the bastard yesterday, right through the neck—*
*won't be messing up my lake front anymore.*

# What Nature Knows

I go down to sit on the shore
near lily pads with yellowed edges.
The rush of wind carries a new freshness,
as it holds its constant conference,
too high in the poplars to distinguish.
I try not to notice the sun has moved
south from its position, but am called to look up
as layers of geese glide high in the sky.
Bluegills no longer congregate above their beds
in the shallows to examine my painted toes,
there are no ospreys to dive feet first,
only the loon pair's offspring, left to fend for itself.
Frogs, out of sight, hold a near-icy silence,
there is only the crickets' rhythmic call, too early in the day,
over and over and over, eager to tell me
what I do not want to know.
Finished, I close my sun-filled book,
holding close its remnants of warmth.

# Parallel Musing

I will not dedicate my poems to you
for you held hard against me my moments to write,
walked away from the first poem shared,
debated the merit of yet another bookcase.

Still, I've heard you whisper, excitedly
*She put on an inch or two,*
saw your bundled body laying
face down on the ice,
large, bare hand stroking her
frigid, pale powder, your dedication
reflected in her glassy countenance.

So, can you not be happy I keep myself amused?
For while you cast in frozen solitude,
I fish for words.
I dedicate my heart to you,
but I will not dedicate
my poems to you.

# Cabin Fever

His snow shoes crush a path
through thigh-high drifts.
He stops to inspect rabbit tracks,
bits of bone, broken branches.
He doesn't respond when she points to
the periwinkle sky, and snow that stays clean.
He doesn't reply when she asks
if she talks too much.

She sings folksongs out loud because she can up here,
heeds the sun's new position, falls behind to listen
to the last of winter's stillness, and with eyes closed,
can almost feel the rush of spring.
She reaches with a branch to write the names
of their children and grandchildren in a smooth
sunny strip of snow, along the trail cut between red pines,
names that will only be seen by the wind that erases them.

On the way back they trace the same path.
He stops to listen to the season's first robin,
and spots both of their names encased in a heart.
He stares a long while, grabs a stick, draws
an arrow head on one side, fletching on the other,
and in silence turns, and continues on.

# Migrations

You tersely admonished
I refused to retain
how to work the woodstove,
instructed again at length,
quizzed doggedly the terms.
Not *vowels*, you said, slipping a pill
under your tongue, *volatiles,*
*volatile organic compounds.*
I owe you my attention, you scolded.
I smiled to myself, as I saw vowels
i, o, and u, floating up the stove pipe.
I tried harder to appease and gently reminded you
I *have* learned the songbird's names,
I *have* learned their many calls,
I *have* learned your woodsman ways.

Today I top loaded the logs,
opened wide the primary air,
engaged the catalytic element
into its secondary combustion,
felt the familiar wave of heat
blanket the cabin and release me.
Only then could I return
to my post at the window.
So stark and cold the leafless birch,
so dark the thistle seeds that fell
from the feeder and peppered
the porcelain snow below,
like the black whiskers you left
in the bathroom sink.

Pine grosbeaks picked at the seeds, looked around,
nervous that dusk would overtake them.
But among them I spotted that curious, lone robin
you said stayed too long into winter's chill
look up and trill *cheer-up, cheerily,*
*cheer-up cheerily, cheer-up cheerily,*
as he flew away.

# Metamorphosis

An old man stares from his porch chair
at silver spangles set onto
checked wings of black and ochre
at rest on the bloom of a coneflower.
He sees his open onion skin hand
transform to a childish palm
lowered into the leafy loam,
where a plump caterpillar wobbles aboard
and tickles a path to his mother's mason jar.

As the old man watches the butterfly
at rest on the bloom of a coneflower,
he sees through widened boyish eyes
that barely clear the kitchen counter,
a grey shriveled sack give way
to radiant wings that when released,
flit to the nectar of the nearest flower,
and he to his trusty, rusty bike
that wobbles and wavers just before
it takes flight.

# A Towhee's Sojourn

Was it a broken leg, wing
or bleak, boundless cold
that led you from the flock
to spend hours, days, weeks
on a pedestal of cracked corn
and black oil sunflower seed
in a world gone glacial?

Did you shelter these north woods nights
under the abandoned cottage next door,
its brown bed shed from pine and oak,
or under the eves of Spencer's summer home
they too worn to return these past years?

The deer came as usual,
lowered their heads to the hay
below your small dark form
your white chest, your rufous wings.
The crows consulted in kind,
dove for seed from naked branches
and bulleted up as blue jays jeered.
Why so quiet, so still on your podium?

Still, like a grainy old photo from
the breakfast window screen,
tiny from the treadmill,
wondrous from my reading chair,
company in my kitchen.
When the weather reached 27 below
did you try to fly south
or succumb—a little life unnoticed,
but significant to me.

# On Her Birthday: A Summer's Song

I awoke to a brush on my cheek
carried on the current of pine boughs
that swayed from narrow trunks
to coax the wind's crescendos
into a bright summer's song.
My mother, gone for decades,
unfurled a sleepy sanctuary
found only in a parent's home,
that took me back to her naugahyde recliner
scented faintly of sunscreen,
feet up, her granddaughter cradled
on its corduroy arm cover
while that same sonata played
through the trees of the lake,
now somber with her news.

# A Moment's Embrace

The sun's glint
   off a polished paddle

the periphery of the lake
   so familiar

the thick dragonfly buzz
   past the ear

the water's slap
   on the keel

the sun-glow drop
   in the trees

the caress
   of a waning wind

the call
   of the day's last crow

the water
   now indigo ink

the embrace
   of a balmy night.

# Lineage

I am the squirt of a sweet tomato
on the bulbous belly of an aubergine
that pairs well with salty chunks of asiago.
I am a useful culinary herb, golden oregano,
with well-rounded leaves that spread
from coast to coast.
I am from Vince of Sicily and Olive of England,
but mostly from Grandma Rose,
who carefully detailed the family lineage
with hand drawn diagrams that stretched
back to the Mayflower, long before
she was given away by her father,
long before she lost her mother,
who died the moment Rose
took her first breath.
I am from those who do not remember
what they were told,
and from those who were told
nothing.

# As I Sail By

The wind strokes velvet fields of wheat,
sends restless leaves about my feet,
promised to fill me, lock to key,
I have the wind, the wind has me.

The sea soothes and smooths its rugged shore,
frightens me with its ominous roar,
promised to feed me, sap to tree,
I have the sea, the sea has me.

Autumn leaves blend in the motion of flight,
color wheel spins into cleansing white light,
an osprey lets out a jubilant cry,
as I sail by, as I sail by.

# About the Author

Nancy Austin was born in Whitefish Bay, WI, but has lived on both coasts, and points in between. She holds a master of science in psychology, and ran a Community Support Program for individuals with mental illness, for many years.

Nancy retired early to move to the north woods near Minocqua, WI, a place she had visited as a child. Its forested geography and abundant lakes draws artists and writers to the area. Nancy relishes time to write in between operating an unofficial bed and breakfast on Bear Lake, where she melds with her blended family, salty second husband, and friends.

She has been published in various literary journals including *Adanna, Midwestern Gothic, Sheepshead Review, Verse Wisconsin* and the *Wisconsin Poets' Calendars*.

❦